I0164221

FR. RANIERO CANTALAMESSA

O.F.M. Cap, Preacher to the Papal Household

Opening Address for the
International Alpha Conference

FAITH

which

OVERCOMES

the world

Foreword

I first heard Fr. Raniero Cantalamessa speak at a conference in Brighton in 1991. His talk had a profound affect on me and I have never forgotten it. Since then I have read all his books that have been translated into English, some of them many times over. His life, example, and teaching are an inspiration to millions of people around the world.

In June 2005, it was a great privilege to welcome Fr. Raniero to open our International Alpha conference. His address on that occasion, Faith Which Overcomes the World, has been an inspiration to all of us involved with Alpha and we are most grateful to him for allowing us to publish it in this booklet.

Nicky Gumbel
Holy Trinity Brompton

The presence-absence of Jesus in our time

In his first Letter St. John says: *"This is the victory that has overcome the world, even our faith. Who is it that overcomes the world? Only he who believes that Jesus is the Son of God"* (1 John 5:4-5).

I should like to reflect with you on this faith in Jesus, which has the power to conquer, that is, to save, the world.

The first question to be asked is this: what place does Jesus have in our society and culture? I think we can speak of a presence-absence of Jesus in our time.

At a certain level, in films, novels, and the mass-media in general, Jesus Christ is very much present; He is indeed a "Superstar." In an unending stream of novels, films, and plays, writers manipulate the figure of Christ, sometimes under cover of imaginary and non-existent new documents and discoveries. *The Da Vinci Code* is but the latest and most aggressive episode in the series. It is becoming a fashion; a literary genre. It is trading on the vast resonance of the name of Christ and on all that He means to a large part of humankind, aiming to achieve wide publicity at very little cost. This is literary parasitism! Yet if in some extreme cases (as in the show, Jerry Springer: The Opera, broadcast by the BBC in January 2005) believers react and phone in to protest, some people decry it as intolerance and censorship. In our day, intolerance has changed sides, at least in the West; where we used to have "religious intolerance," we now have "intolerance of religion!"

From this point of view, then, Jesus Christ is very much present and exploited in our culture. But, if we turn to the ambit of faith, where He really belongs, we notice a disturbing absence, or even rejection of Him. First of all among theologians: one theological current today holds that Christ came for the salvation of the Gentiles, not of the Jews (for whom, they say, it is sufficient to remain faithful to the Old Covenant). Another current says that He is not necessary for the Gentiles either, since they, through their religions, have a direct relationship with the eternal Logos, and have no need of any mediation by the Word incarnate or His paschal mystery. We may well ask, for whom then is Christ still necessary?

More troubling is what we observe in society at large, even among those who consider themselves to be "believing Christians." What do "believing Christians," in Europe and elsewhere, actually believe? Most of the time they believe in the existence of a Supreme Being, in a Creator, they believe that something exists beyond the visible universe and beyond death. This is a "religious" faith, not yet the "Christian" faith, which has the person of Christ as its specific object. Sociological surveys point to this fact even in countries and regions of ancient Christian tradition, like the one where I was born in central Italy. Jesus Christ is practically absent in this kind of religiosity. Taking into account the distinction Karl Barth made, we are dealing here with "religion," not with "faith."

The Church is generally accepted and esteemed as a social agency, for her work in favor of peace and social justice, but is ill tolerated or ignored as soon as she starts speaking about Jesus and His Gospel. Ecclesial movements and individuals who dedicate themselves to evangelization and promotion of faith are easily labelled as conservative, reactionary, or fundamentalist.

Faith in Christ in the New Testament

Let us now compare this situation to what the New Testament says. For Paul, faith, which justifies sinners and confers the Holy Spirit (cf. Galatians 3:2), in a word, saving faith, is faith in Jesus Christ, in His paschal mystery of death and resurrection. *"If you confess with your mouth, 'Jesus is Lord,' and believe in your heart that God raised him from the dead, you will be saved"* (Romans 10:9).

What the Apostle was, above all, at pains to proclaim in Romans 3 was not only that we are justified by faith, but that we are justified by faith in Christ; not so much that we are justified through grace, rather that we are justified through the grace of Christ. Christ Himself is the heart of the message, at a deeper level than even faith and grace. In chapters 1 and 2 of his letter, he had set out to show humanity as universally in a state of sin and perdition, and then he has the incredible courage to proclaim that this universal situation has been radically changed *"through the redemption that came by Christ Jesus"* (Romans 3:24).

The affirmation that this salvation is received by faith and not by works is certainly present in the text, and at the time of the Reformation it was the point that most urgently needed to be brought back into focus. But now that we have reached fundamental agreement on this point (see the document issued jointly in 1999 by the Catholic Church and the World Federation of Lutheran Churches), we are challenged to rediscover and together proclaim what was the fundamental point in Paul's teaching: the universal relevance of Christ's redemption.

No less strong than Paul, is the apostle John on this point. For him, as we have heard, the only faith which conquers the world is faith in Christ. The divinity of Christ and hence the universality of His mission and of His salvation, is, according to him, the specific and primary object of belief. "To believe" without further qualification, henceforth means believing in Christ. It can also mean believing in God, but in so far as it was God who sent the Son into the world. Jesus addresses Himself to people who already believe in the true God; all His insistence on faith throughout the Gospel is concerned with faith in His own person and work.

A rapid perusal of the Fourth Gospel, with an eye to faith in Christ's divinity, shows how this is woven into the very fabric of John's account. Believing in Him, whom the Father has sent, is seen as "God's work" that which is pleasing to God, without qualification (cf. John 6:29). Not believing this is consequently seen as "sin" par excellence: "The Counsellor," it is said, "will convince the world of sin" and the sin is: "they do not believe in me" (cf. John 16:8-9).

A clear line is drawn, dividing the human race into two parts: those who believe and those who do not believe that Jesus is the Son of God. Whoever believes in Him will not be condemned; but whoever does not believe is condemned already; whoever believes has life, whoever does not believe will not see life (cf. John 3:18, 36).

Concretely too, as the revelation of Jesus gradually proceeds, we see two bodies of people taking shape. Of the one it is said that "they believed in Him;" of the other, that "they did not believe in Him." Similarly, after His return to the Father, faith in Him was to remain the great watershed in the heart of the human race: on the one hand there would be those who, despite not having seen Him, would believe (cf. John 20:29); on the other would be the world that refuses to believe. Before this distinction, all other previously known ones sink into second place.

The task of the Church today

1. Proclaim Jesus Christ

A simple look at the New Testament shows us, therefore, how far we are from the original meaning the word "faith" has in Christianity. What then shall we do in this "post-Christian" society? Nothing else but what the apostles and the first disciples did in their "pre-Christian" society! Proclaim Jesus Christ! Proclaim the message, welcome or unwelcome, insist on it (cf. 2 Timothy 4:2). Give back to Christ the place, which is His in faith. Repeat with Paul: *"We preach a crucified Christ"* (1 Corinthians 1:23); *"We proclaim Jesus Christ as Lord"* (2 Corinthians 4:5).

If you go into St. Peter's Square in Rome, your eye is immediately drawn to the obelisk at the center. From whatever point you take in the view, the obelisk always draws the eye: like the mainmast of a yacht, it gives balance to the whole. Jesus Christ is the obelisk at the center of the church; it is to Him that all eyes should always be turned, and to Him that Christians should make people attentive.

This is a task, which no Church can accomplish alone; we need to unite our efforts and resources. Competition and rivalry in this field is a scandal no longer justified by any objective reason. The crucial issue at the beginning of the third millennium is no longer the same that led to the separation of East and West at the beginning of the second millennium, nor is it the same that later led to the division within Western Christianity between Protestant and Catholic.

The controversies between East and West were about the doctrine of the Filioque (whether the Holy Spirit proceeds from the Father alone, or from the Father and the Son), whether to use leavened or unleavened bread for the

Eucharist, and whether to omit the Alleluia or sing it during Lent. Can we say that these are still issues of vital concern to those to whom we must proclaim the Gospel today?

The questions that provoked the separation from Rome of the Churches born of the Reformation during the sixteenth century were chiefly those of indulgences and how sinners are justified. But again, can we really say that these are problems by which today the faith of the people will stand or fall? At a conference held at the Pro Unione Centre in Rome, Cardinal Walter Kasper very rightly drew attention to the fact that, whereas for Luther the primary existential problem was how to overcome the pervading sense of guilt and gain God's benevolence, however, today the problem is exactly the opposite: how to give back to the people of today that true sense of sin which they have totally lost.

In an age in which everyone, from the New Age onward, speaks of salvation as something human beings must find in themselves, how are we to proclaim once more Paul's message, *"that all have sinned and fall short of the glory of God"* (Romans 3:23) and that we have need of a Savior? I am a Catholic (and in addition Italian!), but there are times when I wish that God would give us another Luther today, because (certain controversial points aside, which as a Catholic I cannot entirely accept) Luther for me is the man whose faith in Jesus Christ was more rock-solid than granite. It was he who said, "To lose Christ is to lose all. To possess Christ is to possess all: if Christ is mine, I possess all and can find all."

In the tales of medieval battles (including some described by Shakespeare), there always comes a moment when the orderly ranks of archers and cavalry and all the rest are broken, and the fighting concentrates around the king. That is where the final outcome of the battle will be decided. For us too, the battle today is taking place around the king: it is the person of Jesus Christ Himself that is the real point at issue.

The point on which we must therefore concentrate all our attention from now on, is how all the Christian Churches, in fraternal accord, can proclaim the good news in our modern world; where to start from, what method to follow.

If Christianity, as has so rightly been said, is not primarily a doctrine but a person, Jesus Christ, it follows that the proclamation of this person and of one's relationship with Him is the most important thing, the beginning of all true evangelization. To reverse this order and put the doctrines and moral obligations of the Gospel before the discovery of Jesus would be like putting the carriages in front of the railway engine that is supposed to pull them.

In connection with this, a serious pastoral problem now exists. Churches with a strong dogmatic and theological tradition (as the traditional Churches and especially the Catholic Church are) sometimes find themselves at a disadvantage, owing to their very wealth and complexity of doctrine and institutions, when dealing with a society that has in large degree lost its Christian faith and that consequently needs to start again, at the beginning, that is to say, by rediscovering Jesus Christ.

It seems we are still lacking a suitable instrument for coping with this new situation. Owing to our past, we are better prepared to be "shepherds" than "fishers" of men; that is to say, better prepared to feed the people who have stayed faithful to the Church than to bring new people in or to "fish back" those who have wandered away. This shows how urgently we need a new evangelization, which, while being open to all the fullness of the truth and the Christian life, will yet be simple and basic.

This is the reason why I look with interest and appreciation to the Alpha course. It seems to me that it answers precisely this need of ours; the very name shows this. It is not called "the Alpha and Omega course" (as Revelation 1:8 might have suggested) but simply "the Alpha course," because it doesn't claim to lead people from beginning to end in faith; only to help them get acquainted with it, to foster a personal encounter with Jesus, leaving it to other Church departments to develop the newly rekindled faith.

2. A personal relationship with Jesus Christ

Insisting on the importance of a personal encounter with Jesus Christ is not a sign of subjectivism or emotionalism but is the translation, onto the spiritual and pastoral plane, of a dogma central to our faith: that Jesus Christ is "a person." The General Councils of the early church encapsulated the essential aspects of faith in Jesus Christ in three affirmations: Jesus Christ is true man, Jesus Christ is true God, Jesus Christ is one sole person.

We have here a sort of dogmatic triangle, of which the humanity and divinity represent the two sides and the unity of person, the apex. The Council of Chalcedon (a.d. 451) teaches that Christ must be acknowledged as a person, or hypostasis, not separated and divided into two persons, but the unique and identical only-begotten Son, the Word, and our Lord Jesus Christ.

But the dogma of the one person of Christ is an "open structure," that is to say, capable of speaking to us today, of answering to new needs of the faith, which are different from those of the fifth century. Today no one denies that

Christ is "one person." Some, alas, deny that He is a "divine" person, preferring to say that He is a "human" person. But the unity of Christ's person is not contested by anyone. The most important thing today in the dogma of Christ as "one person" is not so much the adjective "one" as the noun "person." To discover and proclaim that Jesus Christ is not an idea, an historical problem, a fictional character, but a person and a living one at that!

Let us recall the most famous "personal encounter" with the Risen Christ, that of the apostle Paul. *"Saul, Saul!" "Who are you, Lord?" "I am Jesus!"* (cf. Acts 9:4-6). The apostle himself, in the Letter to the Philippians, describes this encounter:

But whatever gain I had [that is, being circumcised, of the seed of Israel, a Pharisee, blameless], I counted as loss for the sake of Christ. Indeed, I count everything as loss because of the surpassing worth of knowing Christ Jesus my Lord. For his sake I have suffered the loss of all things and count them as rubbish, in order that I may gain Christ and be found in him, not having a righteousness of my own, that comes from the law, but that which comes through faith in Christ, the righteousness from God that depends on faith-that I may know him (Philippians 3:7-10, English Standard Version, brackets added by author).

I still recall the moment when this passage became an active reality for me. While studying Christology, I did a great deal of research into the origins of the concept of "person" in theology, its definitions and various interpretations. I was familiar with the endless discussions on the unique person and hypostasis of Christ in the Byzantine period, the modern developments concerning the psychological dimension of the person; in one sense I knew everything about the person of Christ. But, at a given moment, I made a disconcerting discovery: yes, I knew all about the person of Jesus, but I did not know Jesus in person! I knew the notion of person better than the person Himself.

It was actually those words of Paul that helped me to grasp the difference. More especially, it was the phrase: "that I may know Him. . ." and, in particular, that pronoun "Him" (heauton, in Greek) which struck me. It seemed to me to contain more truth about Jesus than all the books I had read or written about Him. "Him" means Jesus Christ, my Lord "in flesh and blood."

It is possible to have an "impersonal" knowledge of the "person" of Christ. A contradiction and a paradox, alas, that is all too common! Why impersonal? Because this knowledge leaves you neutral as regards the person of Christ, while the knowledge that Paul had made him consider everything else as loss, as rubbish, and filled his heart with an irresistible yearning to be with Christ, to divest himself of everything, even of the body, to be with Him.

Entering into a personal relationship with Jesus is not like entering into a relationship with anyone you may run into. To be a "true" relationship, it has to lead to recognition and acceptance of Jesus for what He is, that is to say, Lord. In the text quoted above, the Apostle speaks of a "superior," "eminent" or even "sublime" (hyperechon) knowledge of Christ, which consists in acknowledging Christ as one's personal Lord: "Because of the surpassing worth of knowing Christ Jesus my Lord." (The only passage where the singular is used: "my Lord', not "our Lord.")

The personal knowledge of Jesus thus consists in this:

that I acknowledge Him as my Lord and Savior, which is like saying: as my center, my meaning, my reason for living, my purpose in life, my glory, someone to whom joyfully "I surrender all."

Knowing Jesus Christ is like knowing one's own mother. Who knows their mother best? The people who have read all the books on motherhood, or studied the concept of mother in various cultures and religions? Of course not! They who know their mother best are the children who, having outgrown childhood, realize one day that they were formed in their mother's womb and brought into the world through her birth-pangs. They become aware of a bond that is unique in the world, existing between them and her. Often this comes as a "revelation," as a kind of "initiation" into the mystery of life.

So it is with Jesus. We know Jesus for what He really is when one day, by revelation, not now through flesh and blood, as in the case of our mother, but from the heavenly Father, we discover that we have been born of Him, out of His death, and that we exist, spiritually, for Him.

This is what happened on May 24, 1738 to John Wesley, here in London, as he writes in his journal:

> In the evening I went very unwilling to a society in Aldersgate Street, where one was reading Luther's preface to the Epistle to the Romans. About a quarter before nine, while he was describing the change which God works in the heart through faith in Christ, I felt my heart strangely warmed. I felt I did trust in Christ, Christ alone for salvation; and an assurance was given me that he had taken away my sins, even mine, and saved me from the law of sin and death.[1]

John Wesley's brother, Charles, later put this discovery in poetry in a beautiful hymn entitled *Glory to God and Praise and Love*. In it he sings the joy of being allowed to "call the Savior mine."

An anointing of the Holy Spirit

This living and personal knowledge of Christ doesn't come from us, it can't be obtained by way of conquest, but only as a gift of the Holy Spirit. Nobody is able to say, "Jesus is Lord" except in the Holy Spirit (cf. 1 Corinthians 12:3). It is only after Peter on the day of Pentecost has been "filled with the Holy Spirit" that he can proclaim with such boldness: *"Therefore let all Israel be assured of this: God has made this Jesus, whom you crucified, both Lord and Christ"* (Acts 2:36).

There is an essential link between the gift of the Spirit and this living knowledge of Jesus. Nobody can proclaim "Jesus is Lord" unless he or she is moved by the Holy Spirit, and nobody can be moved by the Holy Spirit unless he or she proclaims that Jesus is Lord. This is a fact of experience: the "power of the Spirit" is not given except to those who proclaim Jesus "Lord" in the same strong and absolute sense as St. Paul does in 1 Corinthians 8:5-6. We need to subject everything, literally everything, to Jesus Christ as the "only Lord," and only when we have decided to do that do we experience a new certainty in our life and authority in our ministry.

Here, dear brothers and sisters of the Alpha course, comes the final challenge of this talk. I have spoken earlier of the scarce relevance the person of Christ has in the faith of people around us, but is this a problem which concerns only others, the "people," or does it, at least in a certain measure, concern also us believers and evangelizers? Let us recall to mind the dialogue between Jesus and the apostles at Caesarea of Philippi, and the two distinct questions of Jesus: Who do people say the Son of Man is?; But you, who do you say I am? (cf. Matthew 16:13-15) The most important thing for Jesus was not what the people were thinking about Him but what the apostles thought.

We must repeat the prayer of the apostles: *"Increase our faith"* (Luke 17:5), or the prayer the father of the sick boy addressed to Jesus: *"Lord, I believe, but help my lack of faith!"* (cf. Mark 9:24).

We need "a charismatic faith" in Christ. How can St. Paul include "the gift of faith" among the charisms (1 Corinthians 12:9), when faith is a theological virtue necessary to all, as hope and charity are? St. Cyril of Jerusalem gives the following explanation:

> There is only one faith, but it comes in two kinds. For there is faith with regard to the dogmas . . . which is necessary for salvation . . . But there is another kind of faith, and it is a gift from Christ. For it is written, "and another (may have) the gift of *faith* given by the same Spirit" (1 Corinthians 12:8-9). This faith, given freely by the Spirit as a gift, concerns not only the dogmas, but is also the cause of those marvels that are beyond all the abilities of humankind. The one who has such faith will be able to say to this mountain, *"Move from here to there, and it would move"* (Matthew 17:20).[2]

This is a kind of faith which comes with a special anointing of the Spirit. Some biblical scholars think that this was the principal meaning of the term anointing in the New

Testament and in the early fathers of the Church: being anointed with the oil of faith to see the truth of Jesus and His word.[3]

When a person is under this special anointing he can say with John: *"We believe and we have come to know that you are the Holy One of God"* (cf. John 6:69); *"And we have seen and testify that the Father sent his Son to be the Saviour of the world"* (1 John 4:14). Believing becomes a kind of knowing and seeing, an inner enlightenment. You hear Jesus saying: *"I am the way, the truth and the life. No one comes to the Father except through me"* (John 14:6) and "I am the light of the world" (John 8:12) and you perceive with all your being (not only with your mind) that this is the truth.

Anointed faith is what gives to a speech prophetic power. Let me try to explain how this happens when we preach about the crucified and the risen Lord. While the preacher is speaking, at a certain point, quite apart from any decision of his, he becomes aware of an intervention, as though a signal on another wavelength were coming through his voice. He becomes aware of this because he begins to feel deeply stirred, invested with a strength and an extraordinary power of conviction that he recognizes clearly is not his own. His words come out as incisive, with greater assurance. He experiences a touch of that "authority" that all recognized when they listened to Jesus speaking. The listener is brought to a point of total concentration into which no other voice can reach: he too feels "touched," and often a shiver goes through his body.

At a moment like this, the human speaker and the human voice fade out of the picture, to make way for another voice entirely. Someone has said: "The true prophet, when he speaks, remains silent."[4] The prophet is silent because, at that moment, it is not he who speaks, but another. God says to his prophets, poor sinful human creatures, *"You shall be as my own mouth'"* (cf. Jeremiah 15:19), and the thought of it makes his messenger tremble.

Of course, this doesn't happen at the same level of intensity all the way through; there are special moments. God needs only one phrase, one word. The speaker and the listeners have the feeling that drops of fire mingle at a certain point with the preacher's words and they become white-hot and shining. Of all images, fire is the one that is least inadequate when it comes to expressing this operation of the Spirit. So it was that at Pentecost, He showed Himself as *"tongues of fire"* (Acts 2:3). We read of Elijah that *"he arose like a fire, his word flaring like a torch"* (Ecclesiasticus 48:1, Apocrypha), and in the book of the prophet Jeremiah, God Himself declares, *"'Is not my word like fire,' declares the Lord, 'and like a hammer that breaks a rock in pieces?'"* (Jeremiah 23:29).

The best thing we can do on an occasion like this is to ask God for a new anointing of His Spirit so that leaving this meeting each one can confidently say, with Jesus: *"The Spirit of the Lord is upon me, for he has anointed me to bring the good news to the afflicted"* (Luke 4:18).

What we need to do is simply ask for an anointing before we set out to do any evangelistic work. Many times my prayers have remained unanswered, but very rarely when I asked for the anointing, especially in some circumstances when I felt weak, tired, and completely unable to say anything. I simply say: "Father in heaven, in the name and for the glory of your Son Jesus, give me the anointing of your Spirit so that I may proclaim the gospel with power and gentleness." Why don't we make this prayer together, right now? We all need to be anointed.

There were times when I almost, in a physical way, felt the anointing coming upon me. Feelings were deeply moved, the soul enjoyed clarity and assurance; all trace of nervousness, all fear and timidity disappeared. Certain songs or hymns are particularly helpful in disposing us to receive the power from on high. One of them is the well known song:

Spirit of the living God, fall afresh on me;
Melt me, mold me, fill me, use me.
Spirit of the living God, fall afresh on me.

There is no counting the number of people who have experienced the anointing of the Spirit coming upon them, while the strains of this hymn and its simple melody rose all around. Why then don't we now sing all together, at the top of our voice and with an expectant faith, this ecumenical tune?

Notes

1. John Wesley, "Journal," *Selected Writings and Hymns,* (New York: Paulist Press, 1981), p. 107.

2. St. Cyril of Jerusalem, Catecheses, V, 10-11.

3. Cf. I. de la Potterie, "L'unzione del cristiano con la fede," in *Biblica* 40 (1959): p. 12-69.

4. Philo of Alexandria, Quis rerum, 266, in Les oeuvres de Philon d'Alexandre, vol. 15, Paris 1966, p. 300.

What is Alpha?

Alpha is a 15-session, practical introduction to the Christian faith designed primarily for non-churchgoers and new Christians. It was developed in London at Holy Trinity Brompton church, and designed as an educational tool for the parish to teach the basics of the Christian faith.

Today, more than 8 million people all over the world have completed Alpha in churches, homes, schools, universities, and prisons. It is supported by all the main Christian denominations, and from early on has been endorsed by Catholic leaders and run in Catholic parishes. "Alpha for Catholics" is a special ministry of Alpha which can assist you in implementing the standard Alpha within a Catholic parish or organization.

For more information and resources, please contact your National Alpha Office.

If you would like more information about Alpha, please contact the following.

Alpha U.S.A.
2275 Half Day Road
Suite 185
Deerfield, IL 60015
Tel: 800.362.5742
Tel: + 212.406.5269
e-mail: info@alphausa.org
www.alphausa.org
www.alpharesources.org

Alpha in the Caribbean
Alpha Office Chagunas
1 Rene Street
Chagunas, Trinidad W.I.
Face Book: AlphaInTheCaribbean
Twitter: @AlphaCaribbean

Alpha Canada
Suite #230 – 11331 Coppersmith Way
Richmond, BC V7A 5J9
Tel: 800.743.0899
Fax: 604.271.6124
e-mail: office@alphacanada.org
www.alphacanada.org

To purchase resources in Canada:

David C. Cook Distribution Canada
P.O. Box 98, 55 Woodslee Avenue
Paris, ON N3L 3E5
Tel: 800.263.2664
Fax: 800.461.8575
e-mail: custserve@davidccook.ca
www.davidccook.ca

www.ingramcontent.com/pod-product-compliance
Lightning Source LLC
Chambersburg PA
CBHW060551030426
42337CB00021B/4531

* 9 7 8 1 9 3 3 1 1 4 3 8 5 *